Nature-Inspired Innovations

ANIMAL-INSPIRED
ROBOTS

Robin Koontz

Rourke
Educational Media

rourkeeducationalmedia.com

Before Reading:

Building Academic Vocabulary and Background Knowledge

Before reading a book, it is important to tap into what your child or students already know about the topic. This will help them develop their vocabulary, increase their reading comprehension, and make connections across the curriculum.

1. Look at the cover of the book. What will this book be about?
2. What do you already know about the topic?
3. Let's study the Table of Contents. What will you learn about in the book's chapters?
4. What would you like to learn about this topic? Do you think you might learn about it from this book? Why or why not?
5. Use a reading journal to write about your knowledge of this topic. Record what you already know about the topic and what you hope to learn about the topic.
6. Read the book.
7. In your reading journal, record what you learned about the topic and your response to the book.
8. After reading the book complete the activities below.

Content Area Vocabulary

Read the list. What do these words mean?

aquatic
autonomous
bioartificial
exoskeleton
humanoid
microbiotics
paralyzed
polymer
submersibles
synthetic
terrain

After Reading:

Comprehension and Extension Activity

After reading the book, work on the following questions with your child or students in order to check their level of reading comprehension and content mastery.

1. Why do robotic engineers look to nature for ideas? (Summarize)
2. What are the advantages of using robotic surgery? (Infer)
3. What is an example of a bio-inspired robot that can go where humans can't go? (Asking Questions)
4. What other tasks do you think the LS3 can help with? (Text to Self Connection)
5. What animals inspired the different ways drones fly? (Asking Questions)

Extension Activity

What familiar animal gives you ideas for things a robot could do? Name one or more animal traits and incorporate them into an idea for a robot that could perform a task that could be helpful to people.

Table of Contents

Animal-Inspired Bots to the Rescue!

One of the most dangerous and difficult jobs is searching collapsed buildings after a disaster. People who are trapped may only have hours to live.

Meanwhile, rescuers must sift, remove, and search through piles and piles of unstable debris to find them. Luckily, a snake might soon be employed to help with the job.

Volunteers from the Turkish AKUT Search and Rescue Association work to locate victims after a structural disaster.

A team at Stanford University is developing a search and rescue soft snake robot. The flexible robot has a pump at one end and a camera at the other. The robot's mechanism allows the robot to slither and squeeze through tiny spaces to search for and reach survivors. It can even deliver supplies while the victim waits to be recovered.

Everything that exists today in nature is the result of billions of years of evolution, tested against the elements and optimized by survival of the fittest. Nature is the world's largest science and engineering lab with 3.8 billion years of experience.

A snake can get into a tight space by bracing the back portion of its body as it pushes and extends the front.

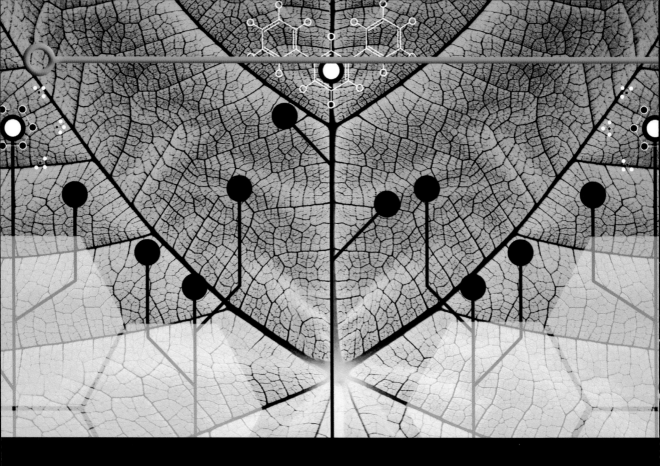

Biomimicry involves studying the way functions are delivered in biology and then translating that into designs that suit human needs. Scientists and engineers involved in biomimicry are often referred to as "biomimics"—people who learn from and attempt to mimic ways that nature has evolved to survive and thrive on Earth for millions of years.

Human-inspired robots with high-functioning hands can use human tools and often perform tasks better and more efficiently than humans, especially in dangerous situations.

They study and learn from nature to create innovative designs that help solve problems in our human societies and improve the world. Robotics is one of the most exciting fields where scientists and engineers have been inspired by ideas from nature. In addition to **humanoid** robots that mimic human movement and behavior, many other creatures have provided important contributions to robotics.

Students at the University of California, Berkeley, designed an inexpensive rescue robot that was inspired by a cockroach. Cockroaches are ancient insects that date back more than 300 million years. They are very strong and fast moving.

The robotic DASH is like a cockroach. It is made from recycled electronics and cardboard. Equipped with a built-in camera, the Dash is fast, agile, and nearly indestructible. The Dash could be employed for all kinds of rescue operations without costing a lot of money.

Cockroaches can flip under a crack and disappear in a flash. They grab the edge with hook-like claws on the back legs, swing under 180 degrees, and land upside down. Some geckos use the same escape technique.

The UC student researchers attached Velcro to DASH so that it could perform the same disappearing act.

Researchers at UC Berkeley looked at army ants when they designed VelociRoACH (Velocity Robotic **Autonomous** Crawling Hexapod). Army ants work as a team to help each other navigate as they gather food for their colony. The researchers added a magnetic winch to VelociRoACH.

Now one robot could assist another robot when traveling on difficult **terrain**. Robots cooperating with each other could make it easier to explore disaster areas.

Maple seeds drop from the trees each fall, twirling like silent helicopters and providing inspiration to drone designers.

Drones are unmanned aircraft that are either controlled by a human or are autonomous. Drone designs were inspired by everything in nature from butterflies to maple seedpods.

Drones can maneuver like a dragonfly, zip like a bee, and hover like a hummingbird. Nature has also inspired ideas to make drones perch, crawl, climb, and safely land.

Drones are used in agriculture for tasks such as crop monitoring, spraying, and irrigation.

Drones are often employed for search and rescue missions. Drones are easy to navigate through expanses of rough terrain and tight spaces. They are safer and less expensive than using airplanes

Once a drone locates its rescue goal, it can send the information to human rescuers. The team can then head straight to the site. The drone can also drop supplies while the survivor waits for rescue.

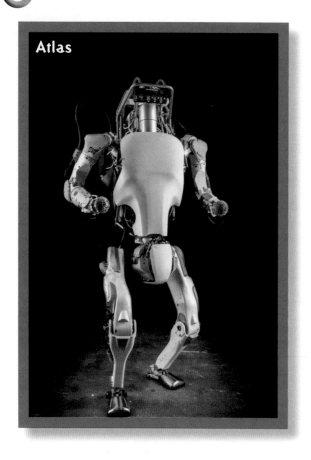

Atlas

Atlas is a bipedal humanoid robot that was designed primarily to assist in search and rescue. Atlas can take care of tasks that are needed in environments too dangerous for humans. Robots have assisted with damaged nuclear power plants and chemical spills.

> **"** By looking to nature, where animals use remarkable combinations of senses, instincts, and body shapes to do amazing things, we can find shortcuts to develop similarly exciting skills for our robots. **"**
>
> *Morgan Pope, mechanical engineer*

At the Fukushima Daiichi Nuclear Power Plant in Japan, engineers employed a small submersible drone called the Manbo to record photos of the damaged reactor.

Medical Bots Inspired by Nature

A new medical robot was designed to move like a snake through the colon. It is equipped with tools and a camera, and a surgeon directs it to perform needed tasks. Thanks to the medical snake bot, complex surgery can be performed inside the colon. Minimally invasive surgery means fewer complications and a quicker recovery.

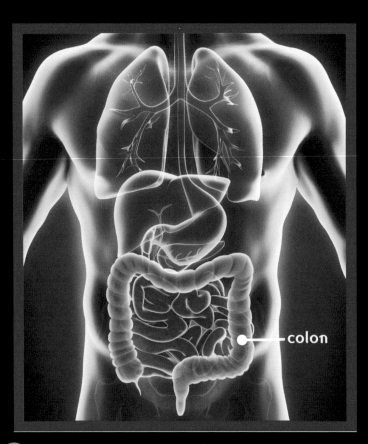

colon

A surgeon can use robotic surgery to operate from outside the operating room with great precision.

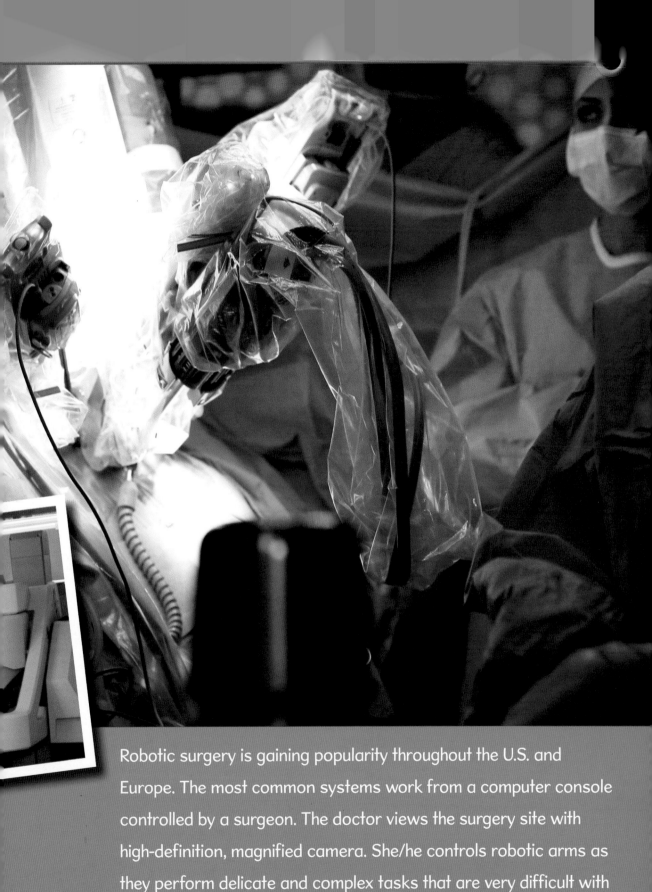

Robotic surgery is gaining popularity throughout the U.S. and Europe. The most common systems work from a computer console controlled by a surgeon. The doctor views the surgery site with high-definition, magnified camera. She/he controls robotic arms as they perform delicate and complex tasks that are very difficult with traditional methods.

Human legs inspired the design of a new **exoskeleton** robot. The wearable robot helps people with weakness in their legs, or who are **paralyzed**.

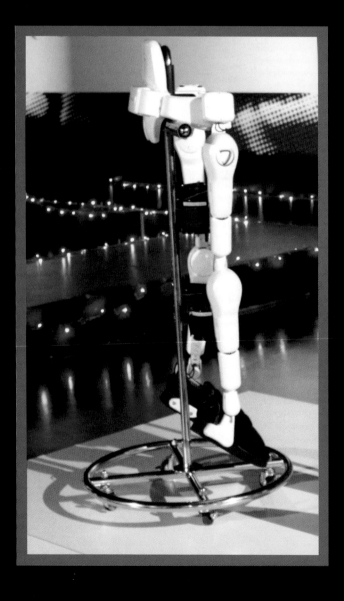

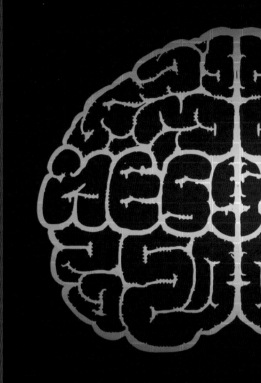

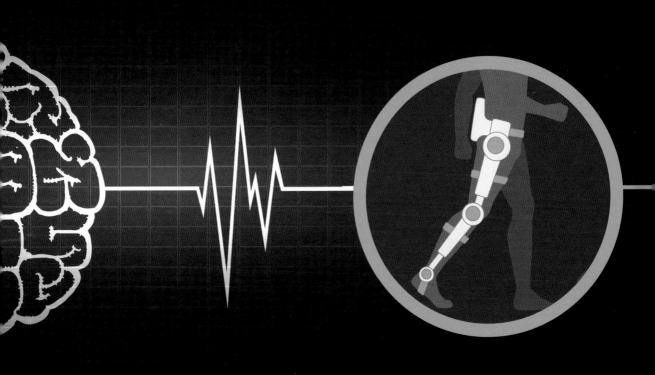

In this new version, the patient's brain signals control the
exoskeleton, just as their brain would normally control their legs.
They improved the knee joint design to be more like an actual knee.
The natural movement makes the robot device more comfortable
and easy to use.

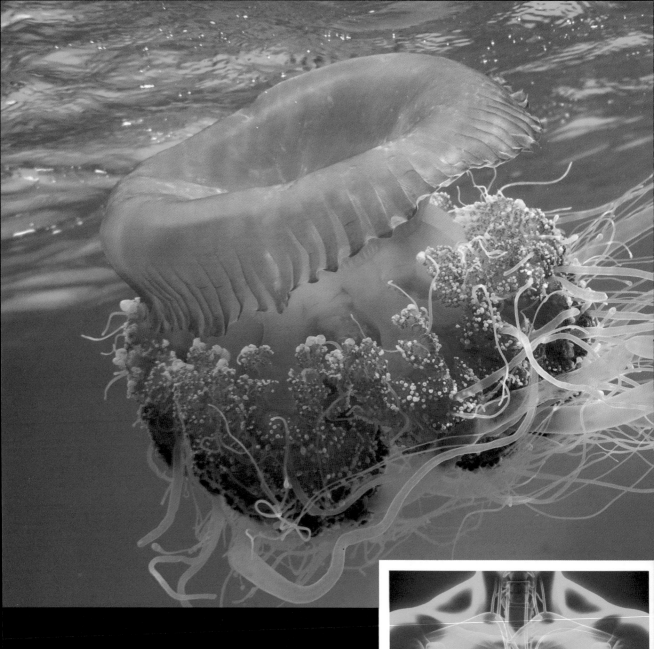

Kevin Kit Parker is working to build a human heart. He was first inspired by jellyfish. The way jellies steadily pulse reminded him of a beating heart. He created a muscular pump that works like a pulsing jellyfish.

Later he improved the system, thanks to inspiration from stingray muscles. While these scientists have a long way to go, inspiration from sea creatures has given them new and innovative ideas to learn and improve the design of **bioartificial** hearts.

Kevin Kit Parker was inspired by the way a stingray flicks one side of its body to change direction.

Biomimetic Bots in the Military

Some of the most advanced robots were originally designed for military purposes. A lot of them are secret, but others have been made public. Many have been adapted for other useful applications.

An operator uses a video game controller and a radio link to operate Spot, a 160-pound (73 kilogram) robot that can be used for tasks such as scouting ahead or carrying loads.

Dragonflies, water striders, and flies have all contributed to the design of micro air vehicles (MAV). Developers at Harvard **Microrobotics** Laboratory designed the tiny RoboBee. It will be employed to record and transmit sensitive data without being noticed.

Eijiro Miyako and his team at the National Institute of Advanced Industrial Science and Technology in Japan have also developed a robo-bee.

They hope to use their design to make a drone that can transport pollen between flowers. It's an example of how robots developed by the military wind up being used for peaceful efforts.

U.S. military engineers are working on insect-like robots that can potentially spy on enemies and carry out missions that could be dangerous for humans.

Researchers for the military hope to design systems for micro aerial robots that make them able to navigate and avoid obstacles. The systems would have the ability to quickly find their way into a structure, send information out, and get out of the structure. It would even hover to defend a soldier's location and keep watch while the soldier performs tasks.

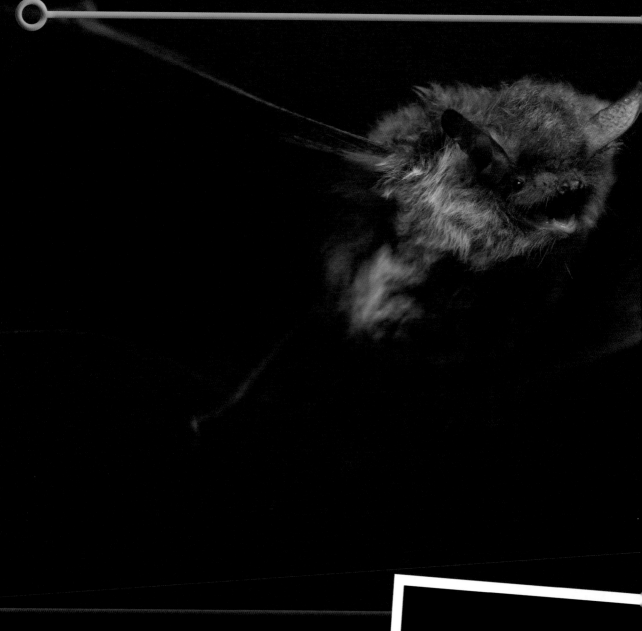

The membrane of bat wings inspired researchers at the University of Southampton in England. They designed thin, flexible wings that work like real bat wings. The controllable wings vibrate as air passes over them.

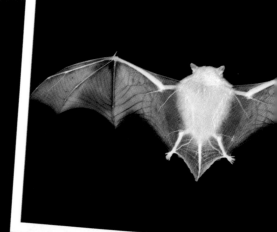

This makes them easier to control and more agile. They installed the wings into a small robotic watercraft. The wings allow the bot to skim quickly over water for long distances while carrying supplies.

The wings on the bat-inspired watercraft can be adjusted through changes in voltage to alter their performance.

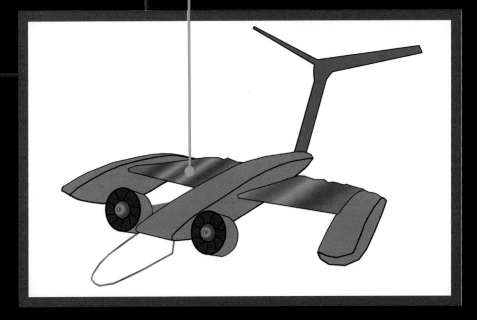

LS3 is a robotic pack animal developed for military use. LS3 stands for Legged Squad Support System. It moves like a four-legged animal through rough and wet **terrain**. The sturdy, headless mule-like creature can carry 400 pounds (181.4 kilograms) of equipment. It can keep walking for 20 miles before running out of fuel.

Designed to go anywhere soldiers travel on foot, LS3 shows its trekking and hauling skills at the Kahuku Traning Area. It was developed by a diverse team of engineers and scientists for Boston Dynamics.

The military decided not to use any of the pack robots they developed because the robots were too noisy! However, the robot creatures taught engineers a lot of about autonomous technology.

Looking like something between a shark and a tuna, the GhostSwimmer can operate in water from 10 inches (25.4 centimeters) to 300 feet (91.4 meters) deep, using its tail for control and forward movement.

The military also funded the design of GhostSwimmer, a drone that looks and moves like a shark. GhostSwimmer can dive down to 300 feet (91.4 meters) and looks a lot like the native sea population. It can potentially be used to inspect ship hulls as well as locate and retrieve equipment. GhostSwimmer or something similar to it could also be used for intelligence missions.

bull shark

Undersea Bots

So far only about five percent of the world's oceans have been explored. While autonomous underwater vehicles (AUVs) have been employed for ocean exploration, researchers have created several bio-inspired robots for deep-sea study in places that are not easily reached or otherwise problematic using AUVs.

An agile, boneless octopus can crawl smoothly along on the ocean terrain. It can shorten and tuck its soft arms into small openings. It can even transform itself into different shapes. Researchers in Italy built a squishy **aquatic** robot, nicknamed Octobot. Octobot can crawl on the seafloor, swim, and grasp objects.

A soft-bodied robot such as the Octobot are built of pliable or elastic materials, making them more flexible and able to twist and stretch as well as change in shape or size.

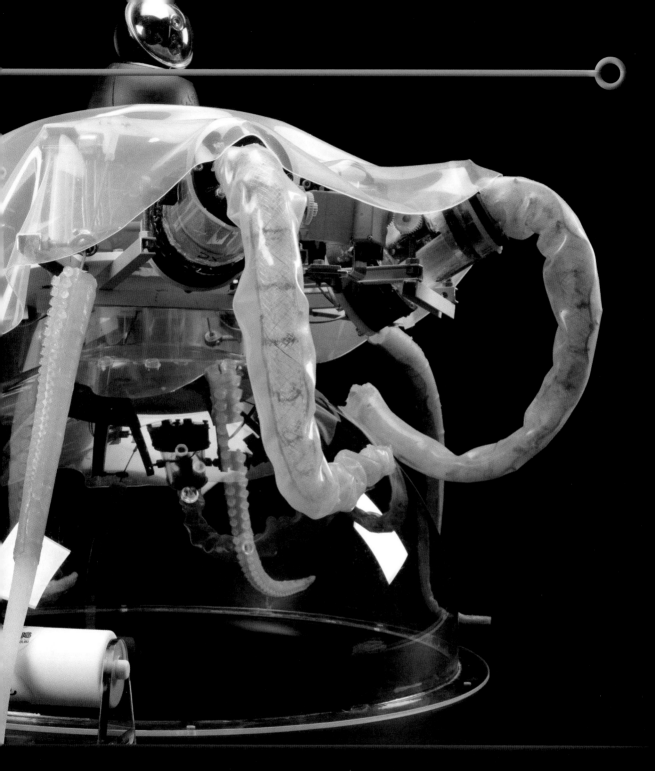

Other researchers have created a **synthetic** skin that mimics an octopus's amazing ability to alter its texture. A robot that can camouflage based on its surroundings could more easily study animals in their natural habitats in secret.

A mussel is a type of marine mollusk with a long, dark shell. A scientist named Brian Helmuth created robomussels. The robots look a lot like mussels and are placed in real mussel beds. Robomussels are equipped with built-in sensing equipment that records temperature.

A global research team has been tracking information from robomussels for 20 years. The database they've created provides information about changes in ocean temperatures around the world.

Numbered and monitored, thousands of robomussels have been recording enormous amounts of valuable data, providing scientists with vital information about marine ecosystems.

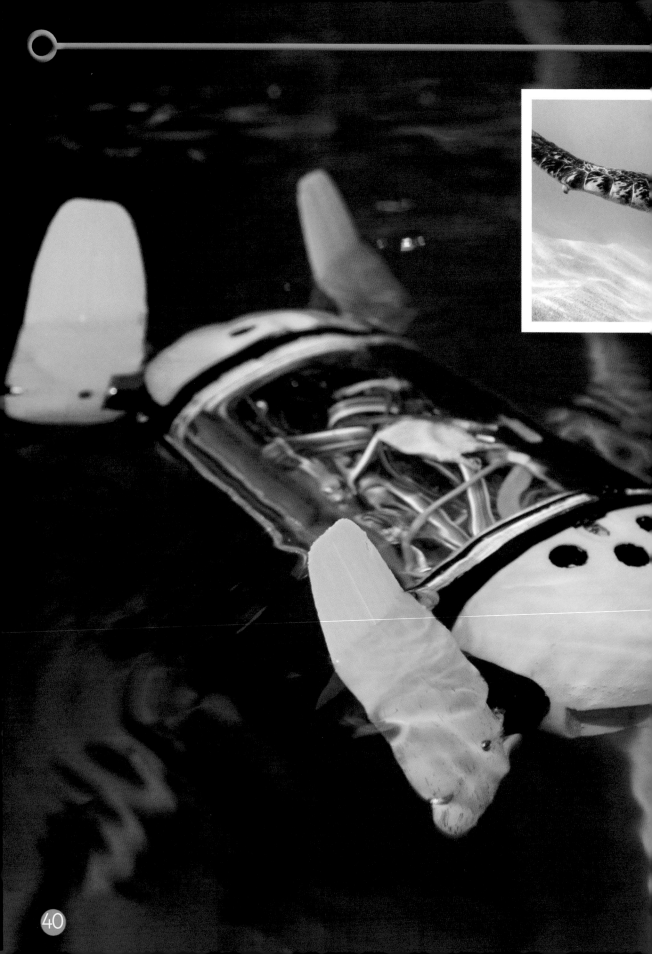

An underwater robot called U-CAT was inspired by sea turtles. U-CAT uses four flippers to swim forward and backward. It can also maneuver in all directions and fit into places where even autonomous **submersibles** can't reach and could be unsafe for human divers. Since U-CAT doesn't use rotors or propellers, is doesn't disturb the water. The water remains clear for U-CAT to take video and photos.

A sea-turtle robot can cost just $70 to build using cardboard and small electronic parts. The design can be made from stronger material if needed. The designers at the University of Arizona hope to send their creation to Mars some day. A similar design is being tested for minesweeping.

The inexpensive U-CAT was designed by Taavi Salumäe, a researcher in the Centre for Biorobotics in Estonia where U-CAT is improved upon and then field-tested in the ocean for deep-sea diving and investigating.

Handy Bio-Helpers

Starfish inspired soft robotic industrial grippers. George Whitesides, of Soft Robotics, created a flexible robotic gripping system. Starfish-like arms made of **polymer** material were pumped with air. Unlike the traditional hard, rigid robotic gripper, his soft, flexible gripper could pick up delicate things without causing any damage. A similar design with rubbery, bright blue fingers is being used in manufacturing and retail plants to pick up and pack just about anything.

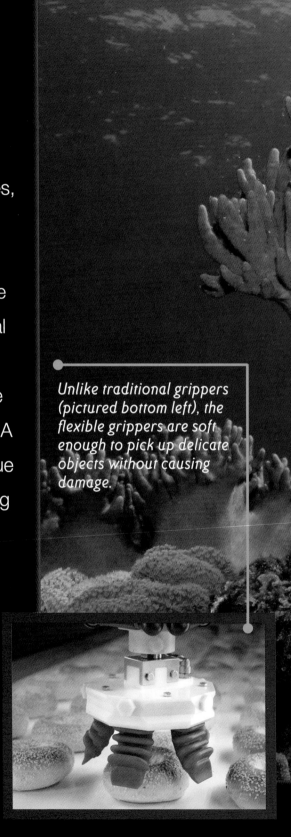

Unlike traditional grippers (pictured bottom left), the flexible grippers are soft enough to pick up delicate objects without causing damage.

66 No starfish has ever tried to lift a pumpkin, but studying how their feet work can lead to robots that can handle awkwardly shaped, delicate objects. 99

George Whitesides

An artist's concept shows how gripper systems will be able to help robotic crawlers like LEMUR (Limbed Excursion Mechanical Utility Robot) inspect the space station's exterior and make necessary repairs.

Geckos can scale vertical walls because of hundreds of microscopic bristles in their toes. Robot scientists created pincers inspired by gecko feet. The robotic grippers stick and unstick using a gentle push. They plan to test their idea on the International Space Station. While robots on Earth are using these grippers, the scientists hope their idea can someday be used to clean up space junk!

Duncan Haldane has worked on several bio-inspired robots. He designed different systems that center on terrain mobility. His robots use bio-inspired features to handle all kinds of landscape challenges. An African bush baby inspired Haldane by the way it could leap. He and his team designed a little jumping robot called Salto.

Salto

Salto can jump three feet (0.91 meters) into the air and keep on jumping. Robots like Salto will be able to spring across terrain that is otherwise difficult or impossible to travel.

Nature continues to inspire and provide ideas to robot scientists as they pursue more innovative ways to create robots.

Glossary

aquatic (uh-KWAT-ik): living or growing in water, as in aquatic plants

autonomous (aw-TAWN-uh-muhss): not subject to control from the outside; independent

bioartificial (bye-oh-ar-ti-FISH-uhl): artificial with natural components

exoskeleton (ek-soh-SKEL-uh-tuhn): a rigid external body covering that provides support and protection

humanoid (HYOO-muhn-noid): having an appearance or character resembling that of a human

microbiotics (mye-kruh-bye-OT-iks): the study of the microbial cells in the human body

paralyzed (PA-ruh-lized): unable to function

polymer (POL-uh-mur): a compound made of small, simple molecules linked together in long chains of repeating units

submersibles (suhb-MUR-suh-buhls): vessels designed to operate underwater, such as for research or exploration

synthetic (sin-THET-ik): something that is manufactured or artificial rather than found in nature

terrain (tuh-RAYN): ground, or land

Index

Show What You Know

1. What are three kinds of robotic movements that were inspired by animals?
2. What animal traits make drones an easier way to search for people?
3. What animals inspired the design of the LS3 and why was it created?
4. What features of a sea turtle inspired biomimicry?
5. What did robot engineers discover about an octopus that would be useful?

Further Reading

Becker, Helaine, *Zoobots: Wild Robots Inspired by Real Animals*, Kids Can Press, 2014.

Benyus Janine, *Biomimicry: Innovation Inspired by Nature*, Harper Perennial, 2002.

Mara, Wil, et al, *Innovations from Nature*, Cherry Lake Publishing, 2014.

About the Author

Robin Koontz is a freelance author/illustrator of a wide variety of nonfiction and fiction books, educational blogs, and magazine articles for children and young adults. Her 2011 science title, *Leaps and Creeps - How Animals Move to Survive*, was an Animal Behavior Society Outstanding Children's Book Award Finalist. Raised in Maryland and Alabama, Robin now lives with her husband in the Coast Range of western Oregon where she especially enjoys observing the wildlife on her property. You can learn more on her blog: robinkoontz. wordpress.com.

Meet The Author!
www.meetREMauthors.com

© 2019 Rourke Educational Media

www.rourkeeducationalmedia.com

PHOTO CREDITS: Cover: model heart © The World in HDR, drone © KSander, hummingbird © kojihirano, jellyfish © Chai Seamaker; pages 4-5 © deepspace; page 6-7 snake © Wichatsurin; pages 8-9 © © GiroScience, Gorodenkoff, Halfpoint; page 10-11 © Lamyai; page 12-13 operating drone © leungchopan maple seed pod © Gavran333; page 14-15 © Suwin, dragonfly © Ger Bosma Photos; page 16-17 ; drone over ocean © Alexander Kolomietz, drone landed © unterwegs, first aid © Fineart1, over forest © PixOne; page 20-21 doctors © Master Video, colon © Nerthuz; page 22-23 brain illustration © Titima Ongkantong, illustration of man © chombosan; page 24-25 heart inside body © Nerthuz, stingray © ovbelov, jellyfish © Chai Seamaker; page 28-29 penny © KWJPHOTOART   , kosmos111; page 34-35 shark © Fiona Ayerst; page 38-39 © Bildagentur Zoonar GmbH; single mussel © zcw; page 40-41 sea turtle © Shane Myers Photography, page 42-43 blue starfish © blue-sea.cz, page 42 yellow robot arm © SvedOliver; page 44 gecko feet © Mr.B-king, All images from Shutterstock.com except: pages 6-7 vine robot © Linda A. Cicero / Stanford News Service; page 10-11 DASH © https://www.flickr.com/photos/solarbotics/17908183829/in/photolist-wA2yLW-wQk7ow-vVL2PM-wQjnFs-U5ggwC-TDXuRx-wA99cv-wA2z9Y-vVLkLi-QibYS1-wAakHp-vVCxqh-vVM3Zv-wSDALK-wA2YJf-wQk6Xw-vVCjLE-vVCe9h-wA9XTc-wTapMM-wSDd1p-wRUBBL-wA2CiU-wRUrnh-vVBKS3-wA2h5Q-wT9Z2e-wSCQoM-wA2kYu-wSCLue-vVBAUJ-wT9ScH-vVLbq4-vVL9XV-vVL8sF-wQiZpd-wT9zNk-vVBfJy-wT9wMR-wT9vqx-wSCmLc-wRTPhw-wQiKDY-wRTHbd-wA1zAU-wSCb76-tKZ3JR-tKZ2Zz-thu89a-864NzU; page 12 ants © Mehmet Karatay   https://creativecommons.org/licenses/by-sa/3.0/deed.en ; page 18-19 Atlas robot http://www.kansascity.com/news/business/technology/917xpi/picture62197987/ALTERNATES/FREE_640/atlas%20from%20boston%20dynamics https://creativecommons.org/licenses/by-sa/4.0/deed.en; Rubble at Fukushima IAEA Imagebank https://creativecommons.org/licenses/by-sa/2.0/; page 22 © Cyberdyne Studio   https://creativecommons.org/licenses/by-sa/2.0/; page 28-29 courtesy U.S. Marine Corps, dragonfly courtesy of U.S. Army; page 32-33 legged robot courtesy of United States Marine Corps.; page 34-35 courtesy of the U.S. Navy; page 37 octobot © Jennie Hills, The Science Museum; Page 40-41 UCAT courtesy of Centre for Biorobotics, Talinn University of Technology https://creativecommons.org/licenses/by/2.0/; page 42 robotic gripper © Soft Robotics Inc.; page 44 inset image of robot courtesy of NASA/JPL-Caltech; page 45 SALTO robot image provided by the University of California, Berkeley;

Edited by: Keli Sipperley

Produced by Blue Door Education for Rourke Educational Media. Cover and Interior design by: Nicola Stratford   www.nicolastratford.com

Library of Congress PCN Data

Animal-Inspired Robots / Robin Koontz
 (Nature-Inspired Innovations)
 ISBN 978-1-64156-457-1 (hard cover)
 ISBN 978-1-64156-583-7 (soft cover)
 ISBN 978-1-64156-700-8 (e-Book)
Library of Congress Control Number: 2018930485

Rourke Educational Media
Printed in the United States of America, North Mankato, Minnesota